50 The Art of Japanese Home Cooking Recipes

By: Kelly Johnson

Table of Contents

- Chicken Teriyaki
- Beef Sukiyaki
- Shrimp Tempura
- Tonkatsu
- Miso Soup with Tofu
- Oyako Donburi
- Ramen with Shoyu Broth
- Udon Noodles with Tempura
- Salmon Miso Yaki
- Gyoza
- Tamagoyaki
- Tonkotsu Ramen
- Matcha Cheesecake
- Chawanmushi
- Okonomiyaki
- Katsudon
- Tofu Steak
- Takoyaki
- Unagi Don
- Yaki Onigiri
- Negimaki
- Miso Glazed Eggplant
- Japanese Potato Salad
- Sweet Potato Tempura
- Gyudon (Beef Bowl)
- Nasu Dengaku (Miso-glazed Eggplant)
- Mochi Ice Cream
- Gyu Don
- Katsu Curry
- Hiyashi Chuka (Cold Noodles)
- Chashu Pork Belly
- Spicy Tuna Rolls
- Matcha Swiss Roll
- Kinpira Gobo
- Goma-ae (Sesame Spinach)

- Inari Sushi
- Shioyaki (Salt-Grilled Fish)
- Japanese Pickles (Tsukemono)
- Ebi Fry (Fried Shrimp)
- Yakitori
- Japanese Curry Rice
- Zaru Soba (Cold Noodles)
- Tofu and Spinach Salad
- Dorayaki
- Nabe (Hot Pot)
- Shabu-Shabu
- Miso-Butter Corn
- Dango (Sweet Rice Dumplings)
- Teriyaki Tofu Stir-Fry
- Japanese Pancakes (Okonomiyaki)

Chicken Teriyaki

Ingredients:

- 2 chicken breasts or thighs, boneless and skinless
- 1/4 cup soy sauce
- 1/4 cup mirin
- 2 tablespoons honey or sugar
- 1 tablespoon rice vinegar
- 2 cloves garlic, minced
- 1 teaspoon grated ginger
- 1 tablespoon sesame oil
- **Chopped green onions** (for garnish)
- **Sesame seeds** (optional, for garnish)

Instructions:

1. In a small saucepan, combine soy sauce, mirin, honey (or sugar), rice vinegar, garlic, and ginger. Bring to a simmer over medium heat and cook for 5-7 minutes, until the sauce thickens slightly. Remove from heat.
2. Heat sesame oil in a skillet over medium-high heat. Add chicken breasts or thighs and cook for 6-7 minutes on each side, or until fully cooked.
3. Once the chicken is cooked, pour the teriyaki sauce over it and cook for an additional 2 minutes, allowing the sauce to caramelize slightly.
4. Remove from heat, slice the chicken, and garnish with green onions and sesame seeds. Serve over rice or noodles.

Beef Sukiyaki

Ingredients:

- **1 lb thinly sliced beef** (such as ribeye or sirloin)
- **1/2 onion, thinly sliced**
- **1/2 cup shiitake mushrooms, sliced**
- **1/2 cup tofu, cubed**
- **1/2 cup bok choy, chopped**
- **1 carrot, julienned**
- **1/4 cup soy sauce**
- **1/4 cup mirin**
- **1 tablespoon sugar**
- **1 tablespoon sake**
- **2 cups dashi broth** (or water with dashi powder)
- **1/2 cup green onions, chopped** (for garnish)

Instructions:

1. In a large skillet or shallow pot, heat the dashi broth over medium heat.
2. Add soy sauce, mirin, sugar, and sake to the broth. Stir to combine and bring it to a simmer.
3. Add the beef slices and cook until they are browned. Then add the onions, mushrooms, tofu, bok choy, and carrot.
4. Simmer everything for about 10-15 minutes until the vegetables are tender and the beef is fully cooked.
5. Serve hot in bowls, garnished with chopped green onions.

Shrimp Tempura

Ingredients:

- 1 lb shrimp, peeled and deveined
- 1/2 cup flour
- 1/2 cup cornstarch
- 1/2 teaspoon baking powder
- 1/4 teaspoon salt
- 1/4 teaspoon white pepper
- 1 egg
- **1/2 cup cold sparkling water** (or regular water)
- **Vegetable oil** (for frying)
- **Tempura dipping sauce** (or soy sauce for dipping)

Instructions:

1. In a bowl, whisk together the flour, cornstarch, baking powder, salt, and pepper.
2. In a separate bowl, beat the egg and then add the sparkling water. Stir to combine.
3. Gradually add the dry ingredients to the egg mixture and gently stir until just combined (the batter should be lumpy).
4. Heat the oil in a deep fryer or large pot to 350°F (175°C).
5. Dip the shrimp into the batter and fry them in small batches for about 2-3 minutes, or until golden and crispy.
6. Remove the shrimp from the oil and place them on a paper towel-lined plate to drain excess oil.
7. Serve immediately with tempura dipping sauce.

Tonkatsu

Ingredients:

- **4 pork cutlets** (preferably bone-in, or use pork loin)
- **1 cup panko breadcrumbs**
- **1/2 cup flour**
- **1 egg, beaten**
- **Salt and pepper, to taste**
- **Vegetable oil** (for frying)
- **Tonkatsu sauce** (or substitute with Worcestershire sauce and ketchup)

Instructions:

1. Season the pork cutlets with salt and pepper.
2. Dredge each cutlet in flour, dip into the beaten egg, and then coat with panko breadcrumbs, pressing gently to ensure an even coating.
3. Heat oil in a deep skillet over medium-high heat (about 1 inch of oil).
4. Fry the cutlets for 5-7 minutes on each side until golden and crispy.
5. Remove the cutlets from the oil and drain on paper towels.
6. Slice the tonkatsu into strips and serve with tonkatsu sauce on the side.

Miso Soup with Tofu

Ingredients:

- **4 cups dashi broth**
- **1/4 cup miso paste** (white or red)
- **1/2 cup tofu, cubed**
- **2 green onions, sliced**
- **1 tablespoon wakame seaweed** (optional)

Instructions:

1. Heat the dashi broth in a pot over medium heat.
2. Add the miso paste to the broth and whisk until it dissolves completely.
3. Add the tofu cubes and cook for 2-3 minutes until heated through.
4. Stir in the wakame seaweed, if using, and cook for an additional 2 minutes.
5. Serve hot, garnished with sliced green onions.

Oyako Donburi

Ingredients:

- 2 chicken thighs, boneless and skinless, cut into bite-sized pieces
- 2 eggs, beaten
- 1/2 onion, thinly sliced
- 1/4 cup soy sauce
- 2 tablespoons mirin
- 1 tablespoon sugar
- 1/4 cup dashi broth
- 2 cups cooked rice

Instructions:

1. In a skillet, heat a little oil over medium heat. Add the chicken and onions, cooking until the chicken is browned and the onions are soft.
2. In a small bowl, whisk together soy sauce, mirin, sugar, and dashi broth.
3. Pour the sauce over the chicken and simmer for 2-3 minutes.
4. Pour the beaten eggs over the chicken and let it cook for about 2-3 minutes until the eggs are set.
5. Serve the chicken and egg mixture over steamed rice.

Ramen with Shoyu Broth

Ingredients:

- 4 cups chicken or pork broth
- 1/4 cup soy sauce
- 2 tablespoons mirin
- 1 teaspoon sesame oil
- 2 garlic cloves, minced
- 2 slices fresh ginger
- **2 ramen noodles** (or any noodles of your choice)
- **Toppings: Soft-boiled egg, green onions, nori** (seaweed)**, bamboo shoots, and cooked chicken or pork**

Instructions:

1. In a pot, combine the chicken or pork broth, soy sauce, mirin, sesame oil, garlic, and ginger. Bring to a simmer and cook for 10-15 minutes to infuse the flavors.
2. Meanwhile, cook the ramen noodles according to the package instructions.
3. Divide the cooked noodles into bowls and pour the hot broth over them.
4. Top with a soft-boiled egg, green onions, nori, bamboo shoots, and any other toppings of your choice.

Udon Noodles with Tempura

Ingredients:

- **2 servings udon noodles**
- **4 pieces tempura** (shrimp or vegetable)
- **2 cups dashi broth**
- **2 tablespoons soy sauce**
- **1 tablespoon mirin**
- **1 tablespoon sesame oil**
- **Chopped green onions, for garnish**

Instructions:

1. Cook the udon noodles according to the package instructions and drain.
2. In a pot, combine dashi broth, soy sauce, mirin, and sesame oil. Bring to a simmer.
3. Divide the noodles into bowls and pour the hot broth over them.
4. Top with tempura and garnish with green onions.

Salmon Miso Yaki

Ingredients:

- 2 salmon fillets
- 3 tablespoons miso paste
- 2 tablespoons soy sauce
- 1 tablespoon mirin
- 1 tablespoon sesame oil
- 1 teaspoon honey

Instructions:

1. Preheat the grill or oven broiler.
2. In a small bowl, mix miso paste, soy sauce, mirin, sesame oil, and honey to make the marinade.
3. Coat the salmon fillets with the marinade and let them sit for 15-30 minutes.
4. Grill or broil the salmon for 4-5 minutes per side, or until the fish flakes easily with a fork.
5. Serve with steamed rice and vegetables.

Gyoza

Ingredients:

- 1/2 lb ground pork
- 1/4 cup cabbage, finely chopped
- 2 tablespoons green onions, chopped
- 1 tablespoon ginger, grated
- 2 tablespoons soy sauce
- 1 tablespoon sesame oil
- 1 package gyoza wrappers
- Vegetable oil, for frying
- **Soy sauce** (for dipping)

Instructions:

1. In a bowl, combine ground pork, cabbage, green onions, ginger, soy sauce, and sesame oil. Mix well.
2. Place a spoonful of filling in the center of each gyoza wrapper and fold the edges to form a pleated half-moon shape.
3. Heat oil in a skillet over medium-high heat. Add the gyoza and cook for 2-3 minutes until the bottom is golden.
4. Add 1/4 cup water to the pan, cover, and steam the gyoza for 4-5 minutes.
5. Serve with soy sauce for dipping.

Tamagoyaki (Japanese Rolled Omelette)

Ingredients:

- 4 large eggs
- 2 tablespoons soy sauce
- 1 tablespoon mirin
- 1 tablespoon sugar
- 1 teaspoon vegetable oil

Instructions:

1. In a bowl, whisk together eggs, soy sauce, mirin, and sugar.
2. Heat a tamagoyaki pan or small non-stick skillet over medium heat and lightly grease with vegetable oil.
3. Pour a thin layer of egg mixture into the pan, swirling to coat evenly. Cook until the edges set but the center is still slightly runny.
4. Roll the cooked portion of the egg into a log and move it to one side of the pan.
5. Pour more egg mixture into the empty side of the pan, lifting the rolled egg to allow the new mixture to flow underneath. Cook and roll again. Repeat until all the egg mixture is used up.
6. Let the tamagoyaki cool slightly before slicing and serving.

Tonkotsu Ramen (Pork Bone Broth Ramen)

Ingredients:

- 4 cups pork broth (tonkotsu broth)
- 2 cups water
- 4 oz ramen noodles
- 1/2 lb pork belly or pork shoulder, sliced
- 2 boiled eggs (soft-boiled)
- 2 tablespoons soy sauce
- 2 tablespoons miso paste
- 1 teaspoon sesame oil
- 1/4 cup green onions, chopped
- 1/2 cup bamboo shoots, sliced
- 1 sheet nori

Instructions:

1. In a large pot, bring pork broth and water to a simmer.
2. Add soy sauce, miso paste, and sesame oil to the broth. Stir to combine.
3. In a separate pot, cook ramen noodles according to package instructions.
4. In a skillet, lightly sear the pork slices.
5. Divide the cooked noodles into bowls and pour the broth over them.
6. Top with pork slices, boiled eggs, bamboo shoots, green onions, and nori.

Matcha Cheesecake

Ingredients:

- 1 1/2 cups cream cheese
- 1/2 cup sugar
- 2 teaspoons matcha powder
- 2 large eggs
- 1/2 cup sour cream
- 1/2 teaspoon vanilla extract
- 1/2 cup graham cracker crumbs
- 2 tablespoons butter, melted

Instructions:

1. Preheat the oven to 325°F (165°C).
2. Mix graham cracker crumbs and melted butter, and press into the bottom of a springform pan to form a crust. Bake for 10 minutes, then cool.
3. In a bowl, beat cream cheese and sugar until smooth. Add eggs one at a time, beating after each addition.
4. Sift matcha powder into the mixture and stir in sour cream and vanilla.
5. Pour the mixture over the cooled crust and bake for 45-50 minutes or until set.
6. Cool in the fridge for at least 4 hours before serving.

Chawanmushi (Japanese Steamed Egg Custard)

Ingredients:

- **2 large eggs**
- **1 cup dashi broth**
- **1 tablespoon soy sauce**
- **1/2 teaspoon mirin**
- **1/4 cup shiitake mushrooms**, sliced
- **1/4 cup cooked shrimp**, peeled and chopped
- **1/4 teaspoon salt**
- **Chopped green onions** (for garnish)

Instructions:

1. Whisk eggs, dashi, soy sauce, mirin, and salt in a bowl until smooth.
2. Strain the mixture to remove any bubbles.
3. Pour the egg mixture into small bowls or ramekins, and place a few pieces of shrimp and mushrooms into each.
4. Cover the bowls with foil or a lid and steam over medium heat for about 15-20 minutes until the custard sets.
5. Garnish with chopped green onions and serve.

Okonomiyaki (Japanese Savory Pancake)

Ingredients:

- 1 cup all-purpose flour
- 2/3 cup water
- 1/2 teaspoon baking powder
- 1 egg
- **1 1/2 cups cabbage**, finely shredded
- **2 green onions**, chopped
- **1/4 cup cooked pork belly**, chopped
- **1/4 cup bonito flakes** (optional)
- **Okonomiyaki sauce** (for drizzling)
- **Mayonnaise** (for drizzling)
- **Oil**, for frying

Instructions:

1. In a bowl, mix flour, water, baking powder, and egg to make a batter.
2. Add cabbage, green onions, pork, and bonito flakes to the batter and mix.
3. Heat oil in a large skillet over medium heat. Pour the batter into the skillet to form a pancake.
4. Cook for 3-4 minutes on each side until golden brown.
5. Drizzle with okonomiyaki sauce and mayonnaise before serving.

Katsudon (Pork Cutlet Rice Bowl)

Ingredients:

- **2 pork cutlets** (tonkatsu)
- **2 cups cooked rice**
- **1/4 onion**, sliced
- **2 large eggs**, beaten
- **1/4 cup dashi broth**
- **2 tablespoons soy sauce**
- **2 tablespoons mirin**
- **1 tablespoon sugar**

Instructions:

1. Prepare tonkatsu by breading and frying pork cutlets until golden and crispy.
2. In a pan, simmer dashi broth, soy sauce, mirin, and sugar. Add onions and cook until soft.
3. Place the tonkatsu cutlet in the pan and pour the beaten eggs over the cutlet.
4. Cover and cook for 2-3 minutes until eggs are set.
5. Serve the tonkatsu and egg mixture over a bowl of rice.

Tofu Steak

Ingredients:

- 1 block firm tofu
- 2 tablespoons soy sauce
- 1 tablespoon sesame oil
- 1 tablespoon rice vinegar
- 1 tablespoon honey
- **1 clove garlic**, minced
- **1/2 teaspoon ginger**, grated
- **Sesame seeds** (for garnish)
- **Chopped green onions** (for garnish)

Instructions:

1. Press the tofu to remove excess water. Cut into thick slices.
2. In a bowl, mix soy sauce, sesame oil, rice vinegar, honey, garlic, and ginger to make the marinade.
3. Marinate the tofu for at least 15 minutes.
4. Heat oil in a skillet and fry the tofu on each side for 3-4 minutes until golden.
5. Garnish with sesame seeds and chopped green onions.

Takoyaki (Octopus Balls)

Ingredients:

- **1 cup takoyaki flour** (or all-purpose flour with dashi powder)
- **1 1/2 cups dashi broth**
- **1 egg**
- **1/2 cup octopus**, cooked and chopped
- **1/4 cup pickled ginger**, chopped
- **1/4 cup green onions**, chopped
- **1/4 cup tempura scraps** (tenkasu)
- **Takoyaki sauce**
- **Bonito flakes**

Instructions:

1. Preheat a takoyaki pan or a cast-iron pan with small round molds.
2. Mix takoyaki flour, dashi broth, and egg to form a batter.
3. Pour batter into the pan, filling the molds. Add octopus, pickled ginger, green onions, and tempura scraps.
4. Cook for 3-4 minutes, then use skewers to turn the takoyaki balls so they cook evenly.
5. Serve with takoyaki sauce and bonito flakes.

Unagi Don (Grilled Eel Rice Bowl)

Ingredients:

- **2 unagi (grilled eel) fillets**
- **1/4 cup eel sauce** (kabayaki sauce)
- **2 cups cooked rice**
- **1 tablespoon sesame seeds**
- **1 tablespoon green onions**, chopped

Instructions:

1. Grill or broil the unagi fillets until heated through, basting with eel sauce.
2. Serve over a bowl of steamed rice.
3. Garnish with sesame seeds and green onions.

Yaki Onigiri (Grilled Rice Balls)

Ingredients:

- **2 cups cooked sushi rice**
- **2 tablespoons soy sauce**
- **1 tablespoon mirin**
- **1 tablespoon sesame oil**
- **1 tablespoon toasted sesame seeds**
- **Nori sheets** (optional)

Instructions:

1. Wet your hands with water to prevent sticking, then shape the rice into small, oval-shaped balls or triangles.
2. Mix soy sauce, mirin, and sesame oil in a small bowl. Brush this glaze onto the rice balls.
3. Heat a grill or non-stick skillet over medium heat. Grill the rice balls, turning occasionally until they are golden and crispy on all sides.
4. Optionally, sprinkle with sesame seeds and wrap with a small strip of nori before serving.

Negimaki (Grilled Beef with Scallions)

Ingredients:

- 1 lb thinly sliced beef sirloin or flank steak
- 1 bunch green onions (scallions)
- 2 tablespoons soy sauce
- 1 tablespoon mirin
- 1 tablespoon sake
- 1 tablespoon sugar
- 1 teaspoon sesame oil
- 1 tablespoon vegetable oil

Instructions:

1. Lay the beef slices flat and place 2-3 green onions at one end. Roll the beef around the scallions to form tight rolls.
2. In a small bowl, combine soy sauce, mirin, sake, sugar, and sesame oil to make the marinade.
3. Place the beef rolls in a shallow dish and pour the marinade over them. Let them marinate for 20 minutes.
4. Heat vegetable oil in a skillet over medium-high heat. Cook the beef rolls for 3-4 minutes on each side, until browned and cooked through.
5. Serve the negimaki with a drizzle of the leftover marinade.

Miso Glazed Eggplant

Ingredients:

- **2 medium eggplants**, sliced into rounds
- **3 tablespoons miso paste**
- **2 tablespoons soy sauce**
- **1 tablespoon mirin**
- **1 tablespoon honey**
- **1 teaspoon sesame oil**
- **Chopped green onions** (for garnish)

Instructions:

1. Preheat the oven to 400°F (200°C).
2. In a small bowl, mix miso paste, soy sauce, mirin, honey, and sesame oil to form the glaze.
3. Arrange eggplant slices on a baking sheet and brush with the miso glaze.
4. Roast in the oven for 20-25 minutes, or until the eggplant is tender and caramelized.
5. Garnish with chopped green onions and serve.

Japanese Potato Salad

Ingredients:

- **4 medium potatoes**, peeled and boiled
- **1/2 cucumber**, thinly sliced
- **1/4 cup shredded carrots**
- **1/2 onion**, finely chopped
- **1/4 cup mayonnaise**
- **1 tablespoon rice vinegar**
- **1 teaspoon sugar**
- **Salt and pepper** to taste

Instructions:

1. Mash the boiled potatoes in a large bowl until smooth.
2. In a small bowl, mix mayonnaise, rice vinegar, sugar, salt, and pepper to create the dressing.
3. Add the cucumber, shredded carrots, and onion to the mashed potatoes.
4. Stir in the dressing and mix everything together.
5. Chill the potato salad in the refrigerator for at least 30 minutes before serving.

Sweet Potato Tempura

Ingredients:

- **2 medium sweet potatoes**, peeled and sliced into thin rounds
- **1 cup tempura flour**
- **1/2 cup cold water**
- **1/2 teaspoon baking soda**
- **Oil** (for frying)

Instructions:

1. Heat oil in a deep pan or fryer to 350°F (175°C).
2. In a bowl, mix tempura flour, cold water, and baking soda to create the batter.
3. Dip the sweet potato slices into the batter and fry them in batches until golden brown and crispy, about 3-4 minutes.
4. Remove from the oil and drain on paper towels. Serve immediately.

Gyudon (Beef Bowl)

Ingredients:

- **1 lb thinly sliced beef (rib-eye or sirloin)**
- **1 onion**, thinly sliced
- **1/4 cup soy sauce**
- **2 tablespoons mirin**
- **2 tablespoons sugar**
- **1/2 cup dashi broth**
- **2 tablespoons sake**
- **Steamed rice**, for serving

Instructions:

1. In a pan, combine soy sauce, mirin, sugar, dashi, and sake. Bring to a simmer.
2. Add the sliced beef and onions, and cook until the beef is tender and the onions are translucent.
3. Serve the beef and onion mixture over bowls of steamed rice.

Nasu Dengaku (Miso-Glazed Eggplant)

Ingredients:

- **2 medium eggplants**, halved
- **3 tablespoons red miso paste**
- **2 tablespoons mirin**
- **1 tablespoon soy sauce**
- **1 tablespoon sugar**
- **1 teaspoon sesame oil**

Instructions:

1. Preheat the grill or oven to 375°F (190°C).
2. Cut the eggplants in half and score the flesh in a criss-cross pattern.
3. Mix miso paste, mirin, soy sauce, sugar, and sesame oil to make the glaze.
4. Grill or roast the eggplants for 15-20 minutes, then brush with the miso glaze.
5. Continue to cook for another 5-10 minutes until the glaze is caramelized.

Mochi Ice Cream

Ingredients:

- 1 cup mochiko (sweet rice flour)
- 1/2 cup sugar
- 3/4 cup water
- 1/2 teaspoon vanilla extract
- Ice cream (flavor of choice)

Instructions:

1. In a bowl, mix mochiko and sugar.
2. Add water and stir until the mixture is smooth.
3. Microwave the mixture for 1 minute, then stir. Repeat 2 more times, microwaving for 1 minute each time.
4. Let the mixture cool slightly, then roll it out between two sheets of plastic wrap into a thin layer.
5. Cut the mochi into small circles.
6. Place a small scoop of ice cream in the center of each mochi piece, then pinch the edges together to seal.
7. Freeze for at least 1 hour before serving.

Gyu Don (Beef Bowl)

Ingredients:

- **1 lb thinly sliced beef**
- **1 onion**, sliced
- **1/4 cup soy sauce**
- **2 tablespoons mirin**
- **1 tablespoon sake**
- **1 tablespoon sugar**
- **1/2 cup dashi broth**
- **Steamed rice**, for serving

Instructions:

1. In a pan, combine soy sauce, mirin, sake, sugar, and dashi broth. Bring to a simmer.
2. Add the sliced beef and onion and cook until the beef is tender and the onions are translucent.
3. Serve the beef and onion mixture over steamed rice.

Katsu Curry

Ingredients:

- 4 chicken or pork cutlets
- 1 cup flour
- 2 eggs, beaten
- 1 cup panko breadcrumbs
- Vegetable oil (for frying)
- 2 tablespoons curry powder
- 1/4 cup soy sauce
- 1 tablespoon mirin
- 2 tablespoons ketchup
- 1 onion, sliced
- 2 carrots, peeled and chopped
- 2 potatoes, peeled and chopped
- 3 cups dashi or chicken broth

Instructions:

1. For the katsu: Dip the cutlets in flour, then egg, and coat with panko breadcrumbs. Fry them in hot oil until golden and crispy, about 4-5 minutes per side. Set aside to drain on paper towels.
2. For the curry: In a saucepan, heat a bit of oil and sauté onions until soft. Add carrots and potatoes, then pour in the broth. Bring to a boil, reduce to a simmer, and cook until vegetables are tender.
3. Stir in curry powder, soy sauce, mirin, and ketchup. Simmer for 10 minutes.
4. Serve the cutlets over rice and pour the curry sauce on top.

Hiyashi Chuka (Cold Noodles)

Ingredients:

- **200g chilled ramen noodles**
- **2 tablespoons sesame oil**
- **1/2 cucumber**, julienned
- **1/2 carrot**, julienned
- **2 boiled eggs**, halved
- **4 slices ham**, thinly sliced
- **2 tablespoons soy sauce**
- **2 tablespoons rice vinegar**
- **1 tablespoon sugar**
- **1 tablespoon sesame paste**
- **1 tablespoon chili oil** (optional)

Instructions:

1. Cook and chill the ramen noodles.
2. Arrange cucumber, carrot, eggs, and ham on top of the chilled noodles.
3. For the dressing, mix soy sauce, rice vinegar, sugar, sesame paste, and chili oil (if using) in a bowl.
4. Pour the dressing over the noodles and garnish with sesame seeds.

Chashu Pork Belly

Ingredients:

- 1 lb pork belly
- 2 tablespoons soy sauce
- 2 tablespoons sake
- 1 tablespoon mirin
- 1 tablespoon sugar
- **1-inch piece ginger**, sliced
- **1 clove garlic**, crushed
- **1 green onion**, chopped

Instructions:

1. Roll the pork belly into a tight log and tie it with kitchen twine.
2. In a large pot, combine soy sauce, sake, mirin, sugar, ginger, garlic, and green onion.
3. Add the pork belly and cover with water. Bring to a boil, then simmer for 1.5 hours, turning the pork occasionally.
4. Remove the pork, let it cool, and slice into thin rounds. Serve in ramen or on rice.

Spicy Tuna Rolls

Ingredients:

- **1/2 lb sushi-grade tuna**, diced
- **2 tablespoons mayonnaise**
- **1 teaspoon sriracha sauce**
- **2 tablespoons soy sauce**
- **1 sheet nori**
- **1/2 cup sushi rice**, cooked and seasoned
- **Cucumber**, julienned

Instructions:

1. Mix the tuna with mayonnaise, sriracha, and soy sauce.
2. Lay out a sheet of nori on a bamboo sushi mat. Spread a thin layer of rice on the nori, leaving a small border at the top.
3. Place the spicy tuna mixture and cucumber in the center of the rice.
4. Roll the sushi tightly, then slice into bite-sized pieces.

Matcha Swiss Roll

Ingredients:

- 3 eggs
- 1/4 cup sugar
- 1/4 cup flour
- 1 tablespoon matcha powder
- 1/4 cup heavy cream
- 2 tablespoons powdered sugar

Instructions:

1. Preheat the oven to 350°F (175°C).
2. Whisk the eggs with sugar until pale and fluffy. Sift in the flour and matcha powder, folding gently.
3. Pour the batter onto a lined baking sheet and bake for 10-12 minutes.
4. While the cake is baking, whip the heavy cream with powdered sugar until stiff peaks form.
5. Once the cake is baked, remove from the oven and cool on a wire rack.
6. Spread whipped cream evenly on the cooled cake, then roll it up. Chill in the fridge for 30 minutes before slicing.

Kinpira Gobo

Ingredients:

- **1 burdock root (gobo)**, julienned
- **1 carrot**, julienned
- **2 tablespoons sesame oil**
- **2 tablespoons soy sauce**
- **1 tablespoon mirin**
- **1 tablespoon sugar**
- **1 teaspoon sesame seeds**

Instructions:

1. In a pan, heat sesame oil and sauté the burdock root and carrot until tender, about 5 minutes.
2. Add soy sauce, mirin, sugar, and continue to stir-fry for 3 more minutes.
3. Sprinkle with sesame seeds and serve.

Goma-ae (Sesame Spinach)

Ingredients:

- **1 bunch spinach**, blanched
- **2 tablespoons sesame seeds**
- **1 tablespoon soy sauce**
- **1 tablespoon mirin**
- **1 teaspoon sugar**

Instructions:

1. Toast the sesame seeds in a dry pan until fragrant. Grind the seeds in a mortar and pestle.
2. Mix the ground sesame seeds with soy sauce, mirin, and sugar to make the dressing.
3. Toss the spinach in the dressing and serve.

Inari Sushi

Ingredients:

- **10 inari sushi pouches**
- **1 cup sushi rice**, cooked and seasoned
- **Sesame seeds** (optional)

Instructions:

1. Gently stuff the inari pouches with seasoned sushi rice.
2. Optionally, sprinkle sesame seeds on top before serving.

Shioyaki (Salt-Grilled Fish)

Ingredients:

- **2 whole fish** (such as mackerel or salmon), cleaned
- **Kosher salt**

Instructions:

1. Sprinkle the fish generously with kosher salt.
2. Grill the fish over medium heat until cooked through, about 10-15 minutes.
3. Serve with lemon wedges.

Japanese Pickles (Tsukemono)

Ingredients:

- **1 cucumber**, thinly sliced
- **1/2 tablespoon salt**
- **1 tablespoon rice vinegar**
- **1 tablespoon sugar**

Instructions:

1. Sprinkle the cucumber slices with salt and let sit for 30 minutes to draw out moisture.
2. Rinse the cucumbers and combine with rice vinegar and sugar.
3. Let the pickles sit for at least an hour before serving.

Ebi Fry (Fried Shrimp)

Ingredients:

- **10 large shrimp**, peeled and deveined
- **1/2 cup flour**
- **1 egg**, beaten
- **1 cup panko breadcrumbs**
- **Vegetable oil** (for frying)

Instructions:

1. Dip each shrimp in flour, then egg, and coat with panko breadcrumbs.
2. Heat vegetable oil in a pan over medium heat and fry the shrimp until golden and crispy, about 3-4 minutes.
3. Drain on paper towels and serve with tonkatsu sauce.

Yakitori

Ingredients:

- **12 chicken thigh pieces**, cut into bite-sized chunks
- **1 green onion**, chopped into 2-inch pieces
- **1 tablespoon vegetable oil**
- For the marinade/sauce:
    - **3 tablespoons soy sauce**
    - **2 tablespoons sake**
    - **1 tablespoon mirin**
    - **1 tablespoon sugar**
    - **1 tablespoon grated ginger**
    - **1 clove garlic**, minced

Instructions:

1. Thread the chicken pieces and green onion onto skewers.
2. In a bowl, combine soy sauce, sake, mirin, sugar, ginger, and garlic to make the marinade.
3. Brush the skewered chicken with the marinade and let it sit for about 30 minutes.
4. Heat oil in a grill pan or barbecue over medium heat. Grill the skewers, basting with the marinade, until the chicken is cooked through and slightly charred (about 5-7 minutes per side).
5. Serve with a sprinkle of sesame seeds and chopped green onions.

Japanese Curry Rice

Ingredients:

- **2 tablespoons vegetable oil**
- **1 onion**, chopped
- **2 carrots**, peeled and chopped
- **2 potatoes**, peeled and cubed
- **1 lb chicken breast or beef stew meat**, cubed
- **4 cups water or chicken broth**
- **1 box Japanese curry roux** (available in stores)
- **Cooked white rice** (for serving)

Instructions:

1. In a large pot, heat the vegetable oil over medium heat. Add the onions and sauté until soft.
2. Add the chicken or beef cubes and brown them on all sides.
3. Add the carrots and potatoes, then pour in the water or chicken broth. Bring it to a boil and then reduce the heat to simmer.
4. Once the vegetables are tender, break up the curry roux and stir it into the pot.
5. Simmer the curry until thickened, about 10 minutes.
6. Serve the curry over a bowl of steamed white rice.

Zaru Soba (Cold Noodles)

Ingredients:

- **200g soba noodles**
- **1/4 cup soy sauce**
- **2 tablespoons mirin**
- **1 tablespoon sugar**
- **1/4 cup water**
- **2 green onions**, chopped
- **1 tablespoon toasted sesame seeds**

Instructions:

1. Cook the soba noodles according to package directions. Drain and rinse under cold water to stop the cooking process.
2. In a small saucepan, combine soy sauce, mirin, sugar, and water. Heat until the sugar dissolves, then let it cool.
3. Serve the chilled soba noodles on a bamboo mat or plate.
4. Pour the dipping sauce into small bowls for each person.
5. Garnish the noodles with green onions and toasted sesame seeds, and dip the noodles into the sauce as you eat.

Tofu and Spinach Salad

Ingredients:

- **200g firm tofu**, cubed
- **2 cups spinach leaves**, washed
- **1 tablespoon sesame oil**
- **1 tablespoon soy sauce**
- **1 teaspoon rice vinegar**
- **1 teaspoon sesame seeds**
- **1 tablespoon honey** (optional)

Instructions:

1. In a pan, heat sesame oil and fry the tofu cubes until golden and crispy, about 4-5 minutes per side.
2. In a small bowl, whisk together soy sauce, rice vinegar, honey (if using), and sesame seeds.
3. Toss the spinach leaves in the dressing and top with crispy tofu cubes.
4. Serve immediately as a light and refreshing salad.

Dorayaki

Ingredients:

- **For the pancakes:**
    - **2 eggs**
    - **1/2 cup sugar**
    - **1/4 cup honey**
    - **1/4 cup water**
    - **1 cup flour**
    - **1/2 teaspoon baking powder**
    - **Butter** (for cooking)
- **For the filling:**
    - **1 cup red bean paste (anko)**

Instructions:

1. Whisk the eggs, sugar, honey, and water in a bowl.
2. Sift the flour and baking powder into the mixture and stir until smooth.
3. Heat a lightly buttered non-stick skillet over medium-low heat. Pour small amounts of batter onto the pan to form pancakes, about 3 inches in diameter. Cook for 1-2 minutes per side until golden.
4. Let the pancakes cool slightly, then spread a spoonful of red bean paste onto one pancake.
5. Place another pancake on top, sandwiching the filling, and press gently to seal.
6. Serve as a sweet snack or dessert.

Nabe (Hot Pot)

Ingredients:

- **4 cups dashi broth**
- **1/2 lb chicken thigh or pork belly**, sliced thinly
- **1/2 lb tofu**, cut into cubes
- **1 cup shiitake mushrooms**, sliced
- **2 cups napa cabbage**, chopped
- **1 carrot**, thinly sliced
- **1 green onion**, chopped
- **1 tablespoon soy sauce**
- **1 tablespoon mirin**
- **1 teaspoon sesame oil**

Instructions:

1. In a large pot, combine the dashi broth, soy sauce, mirin, and sesame oil. Bring to a simmer over medium heat.
2. Add the chicken or pork slices, tofu, mushrooms, cabbage, and carrots into the pot.
3. Simmer for about 10-15 minutes, or until the ingredients are cooked through and tender.
4. Garnish with green onions and serve hot with a side of rice or dipping sauce.

Shabu-Shabu

Ingredients:

- **1 lb thinly sliced beef** (or pork, chicken, or tofu for a vegetarian version)
- **6 cups dashi broth** (or water with 1-2 tablespoons dashi powder)
- **1/2 napa cabbage**, sliced
- **1 cup shiitake mushrooms**, sliced
- **1 cup enoki mushrooms**
- **1 block firm tofu**, cut into cubes
- **1 carrot**, thinly sliced
- **1 cup bok choy**, chopped
- **Soy sauce**, for dipping
- **Ponzu sauce**, for dipping
- **Sesame seeds**, for garnish

Instructions:

1. In a large pot, bring the dashi broth to a simmer over medium heat.
2. Arrange the sliced beef (or protein of your choice), cabbage, mushrooms, tofu, carrot, and bok choy on a platter.
3. Once the broth is simmering, dip the thinly sliced beef (or vegetables) into the broth for 10-20 seconds to cook.
4. Use chopsticks or a slotted spoon to remove the ingredients from the broth. Dip them in soy sauce or ponzu sauce for added flavor.
5. Continue to cook and dip ingredients into the broth until finished. Garnish with sesame seeds and serve with steamed rice.

Miso-Butter Corn

Ingredients:

- **2 cups frozen corn kernels** (or fresh if available)
- **1 tablespoon unsalted butter**
- **1 tablespoon white miso paste**
- **1 teaspoon soy sauce**
- **1/2 teaspoon sugar**
- **1/2 teaspoon sesame oil**
- **Chopped green onions** (for garnish)
- **Sesame seeds** (optional, for garnish)

Instructions:

1. In a medium skillet, melt the butter over medium heat.
2. Add the corn kernels and sauté for about 5-7 minutes until heated through and slightly browned.
3. In a small bowl, whisk together the miso paste, soy sauce, sugar, and sesame oil.
4. Pour the miso mixture over the corn and stir to coat evenly. Cook for another 2-3 minutes until the sauce thickens slightly.
5. Garnish with chopped green onions and sesame seeds, if desired. Serve as a side dish.

Dango (Sweet Rice Dumplings)

Ingredients:

- **1 cup glutinous rice flour (mochi flour)**
- **1/4 cup sugar**
- **1/2 cup water**
- **1 tablespoon soy sauce** (for the dipping sauce)
- **1 tablespoon mirin**
- **1 tablespoon sugar** (for the dipping sauce)

Instructions:

1. In a mixing bowl, combine the glutinous rice flour and sugar. Slowly add water, stirring until a dough forms.
2. Divide the dough into small balls, about 1 inch in diameter.
3. Bring a large pot of water to a boil. Drop the dango balls into the water and cook for about 3-4 minutes until they float to the surface.
4. Remove the dango with a slotted spoon and set aside to cool slightly.
5. In a small saucepan, combine soy sauce, mirin, and sugar to make the dipping sauce. Heat over low heat until the sugar dissolves.
6. Skewer the dango balls onto sticks and drizzle with the dipping sauce. Serve warm or at room temperature.

Teriyaki Tofu Stir-Fry

Ingredients:

- **1 block firm tofu**, cubed
- **1 tablespoon sesame oil**
- **1 bell pepper**, sliced
- **1 small onion**, sliced
- **1 carrot**, julienned
- **1 zucchini**, sliced
- **2 tablespoons soy sauce**
- **2 tablespoons mirin**
- **1 tablespoon sugar**
- **1 tablespoon rice vinegar**
- **1 tablespoon cornstarch** (optional, for thickening)
- **Sesame seeds**, for garnish
- **Chopped green onions**, for garnish

Instructions:

1. Press the tofu to remove excess moisture, then cut it into cubes.
2. In a large skillet or wok, heat sesame oil over medium heat. Add the tofu and cook until golden on all sides, about 5-7 minutes. Remove and set aside.
3. In the same skillet, add the bell pepper, onion, carrot, and zucchini. Stir-fry for 4-5 minutes until tender-crisp.
4. In a small bowl, mix the soy sauce, mirin, sugar, and rice vinegar. If you prefer a thicker sauce, whisk in the cornstarch.
5. Add the tofu back to the pan and pour the teriyaki sauce over the vegetables and tofu. Stir to coat evenly.
6. Cook for an additional 2-3 minutes until the sauce thickens and everything is well combined.
7. Serve the stir-fry over rice, garnished with sesame seeds and chopped green onions.

Japanese Pancakes (Okonomiyaki)

Ingredients:

- 1 1/2 cups all-purpose flour
- 1 cup dashi broth
- 1 egg
- 1/2 cup shredded cabbage
- 1/4 cup chopped green onions
- 1/4 cup cooked shrimp or pork belly (optional)
- 1 tablespoon soy sauce
- 1/2 teaspoon baking powder
- **Vegetable oil**, for frying
- **Okonomiyaki sauce** (or a mix of Worcestershire sauce and ketchup)
- **Bonito flakes**, for garnish
- **Kewpie mayo** (Japanese mayonnaise), for garnish

Instructions:

1. In a large bowl, whisk together flour, dashi broth, egg, soy sauce, and baking powder. Add the cabbage, green onions, and optional shrimp or pork. Mix to combine.
2. Heat a non-stick skillet or griddle over medium heat and add a little vegetable oil.
3. Pour the batter onto the skillet to form a round pancake (about 6 inches in diameter). Cook for 3-4 minutes on each side, flipping carefully, until golden brown and cooked through.
4. Once cooked, transfer to a plate and drizzle with Okonomiyaki sauce and mayonnaise. Garnish with bonito flakes.
5. Serve hot, cut into wedges.

www.ingramcontent.com/pod-product-compliance
Lightning Source LLC
LaVergne TN
LVHW081505060526
838201LV00056BA/2946